DANCE UPON THE FOREST FLOOR

Dance upon the Forest Floor

Poems By

DONNY BARILLA

Adelaide Books
New York / Lisbon
2018

DANCE UPON THE FOREST FLOOR
a collection of poems by
Donny Barilla

Copyright © 2018 by Donny Barilla

Cover image © 2018 A. F. Nikolic

Published by Adelaide Books, New York / Lisbon
adelaidebooks.org

Editor-in-Chief
Stevan V. Nikolic

All rights reserved. No part of this book may be reproduced in any manner whatsoever without written permission from the author except in the case of brief quotations embodied in critical articles and reviews.

For any information, please address Adelaide Books
at info@adelaidebooks.org
or write to:
Adelaide Books
244 Fifth Ave. Suite D27
New York, NY, 10001

ISBN13: 978-1-949180-10-7
ISBN10: 1-949180-10-7

Printed in the United States of America

Geese Fly

Geese flood northern skies
mushrooms crop a blooming glade
her scent lingers slow.

2 / 9 / 1999

To,

Kimbaly Mcdonnell

You've been touched with beauty and a loving heart.

Contents

BY A WOODLAND POND
Refuge from the Rain   *17*
Onset of Day   *19*
Autumn Nocturne   *20*
Fallen Seeds   *22*
A Day in the Pasture   *23*
Alive in the Glades   *24*
Country Dreaming   *25*
Until the Close of Day   *27*
Summer Showers   *28*
Sulking at Nightfall   *29*
Soft Smile   *30*
Hungry Flash   *31*
Clamor the Ground   *32*
Buzz and Steep   *33*
Nibbling Seeds   *34*
Shards and the Crimping Earth   *35*
Down   *36*
Moonlit Leaves   *37*
Elm Leaves   *38*
Fur Trees   *39*
Robins   *40*
Molecules   *41*
From Orchard to Rolling Stream   *42*
Mountain Spring   *43*

Her Summit *44*
Hyacinth *45*
Brittle Winter *46*
Quaking Breads *47*
Distant Shore *48*
Row Boat *49*
Bundles of Yarn *50*
Comforter of Down *51*
April 26, 2016 Pennsylvania Landscape *52*
Drought *53*
Apple Grove *54*
Smooth Water *55*
California Gold *56*
From the Tender Current *57*
FALLEN BLOUSE...
Blouse and Gown *61*
Alone at Midnight *62*
Dreaming in Autumn *63*
Full Moon Naked *64*
Evergreen *65*
Stooped to the Lilac Bush *66*
Daybreak *67*
Cape Cod *68*
Squall *69*
Shoreline *70*
Gilded Rays *71*
Lovemaking in the Winter Hour *72*
At the Machias *73*
Pit and Pail *74*
Summer Heat *75*
Belly Dancer *77*

Scribbles from Hera's Diary *78*
Zeus' Thunderbolts *79*
AS ONE PONDERS THE QUIET THAW
Thaw *83*
Undressing *85*
From the Grave *86*
Waiting for Warmth *87*
Shades of Green *88*
By Lakeside *89*
Scent of Autumn *90*
Milk *92*
Winter Blooms *93*
At End of Day *94*
Swooned in Early Spring *95*
As the Fog Fades *97*
Taking Time *98*
Searching the Pines *99*
Wooded Silence *100*
Breakfast *101*
Fantasy, Pennsylvania 2017 *102*
Robes of Spring *104*
Autumn Compromise *106*
Remembering Youth *107*
The Fountain *109*
Evening Roams *110*
Forever Lost *111*
Oceans Foams *112*
Morning Walk *113*
Shadows *114*
Early Summer *115*
Februaries *116*

Threads of Autumn   *118*

TOKENS ON A GIVEN SEASON

Lost in the Open   *121*

Siren   *122*

Forest Floor   *123*

Edging the Stream   *124*

Summer Love   *126*

Sleeping with Jasper   *127*

Woodlands Come Alive   *128*

Flesh upon the Ocean   *130*

Roses in the Morning Fog   *131*

Awake with Her at Summer's Edge   *132*

Nocturne in a Dream   *133*

Time Spent with Blackbirds   *134*

Beatitudes of a Sacred Earth   *135*

Covered as the Fog Lifts   *136*

Wintery Quilts   *137*

Genesis   *138*

Dead Tongues   *139*

Winter's Gambit   *140*

Cantor in the Deep of Night   *142*

Into the Fey   *143*

Shadows Break at Spring   *144*

Beneath the Pond   *145*

An Evening after a Heavy Blizzard   *146*

Arriving Just before Nightfall   *147*

By River, By Meadow   *148*

Lavender Bush   *149*

Thicket of a Bruising Wood   *150*

Threading My Way   *151*

About the Author   *157*

BY A WOODLAND POND

Refuge from the Rain
dedicated to *The East Penn Diner*

She threw a clever smile while wiping the table dry.
Thunder teased and the thick glass windows shook.
Coffee wrestled down the arid nooks of my throat,
I teased the steam across my lips.

I dove my eyes deep into the freckles of her chest.
Quietly, I gathered her scents-
drifting spices which glanced upon my skin
and lifted to the trembling cauldron of her slow, steady breath
and rose, steam from a rattling plate.

I absorbed the garden of her flesh with my eager pressing lips.
Sinews of her muscled calves crept across her leg.
She danced in her skirt, apron, and blouse.

I begged her slender fingers.
Rain seeped across the cool windows,
puddles gathered the thick pelt of the heaven's water.
I smothered my mouth to steamy food.

Crumbling, I shook to the dance, thickest hunger
so alive and awake her breasts saunter through
the softest, slickest moans.
She gathered each ghost of a wilting hush, the evening
pressed on as it does, thrashing through the night.

Donny Barilla

She turned her soft smiling face.
The register sang notes, hymns,
quick fugues stroked my ears
as eyes cascaded across warm breads, alive with butter.

Onset of Day

The trail stretched, dove through the forest in curves.

As I walked, I draped my hands across the leaves
alive with early green buds.

The earth was soft and catered to the press of my foot.

I could hear the chirp of the morning birds gently fill the
gaps of thin morning air.

Fog stretched like thin cotton, gripping the trees and bushes.

The spread of the silk mist weaved through the ferns, slouching.

I brushed my hands against the elm.

I walked through the bristled branch and twig.

Donny Barilla

Autumn Nocturne

By river's edge, I lay quiet on rock and pastures of mud.

With opened mouth,
the wind and Autumn breath sweep the forest floor

as dust settles on my nape, neck, and parched throat.

My arms, tendrils of fingers scrape the tree trunk and I moan

to the muffled sounds of a distant snow.
My waist threshes to the quivering

bed of pine needles, so gentle the scent of mint seeps
through to my mouth and nostril.

As if the ice of a coming month, gathers in the fat of the gray clouds,

I slumber by this chilled patch of grass
and wait for the frost to spread across

my limbs and burrow through to my burning genitals.
Whip of the groaning geese

DANCE UPON THE FOREST FLOOR

as they tempt their way across the frosted skyline,
fog spreads across my body

as a moistened cream of lavender.
A few weeks later, foams slap the rivers edge.

I lessen my posture and cloak into the breasted mound
of mosses, so alive and yet

fading with the pounce of icy nocturnes
descending from the dancing skyline, so alone

the nakedness of late Autumn.

Donny Barilla

Fallen Seeds

Sweet juices pooled about the floor of my mouth.

I snapped the apples skin and felt the floods slap across my tongue.

Pulps sauteed the parchment walls of my throat

as I opened this rivulet as a gash only to thicken its way

down the beard of my chin, neck. Walking through the grove, I

sat beneath a tree which offered a gown. Quiet shadows of the Autumn

burgundy sun flickered calm dancing lights which rested upon my eager skin.

I wandered through the nearby pasture.

Glazes of fallen leaves and chipped acorns

pressed in anticipation under the thick of my boot.

DANCE UPON THE FOREST FLOOR

A Day in the Pasture

I steep my ankles through the waistline of the tender soils and grasses.

Softly, a field mouse pampers it's way across my boot. The sun

genuflects to the regal awaiting pasture as I watch each beam trembles

through the cottony clouds, dispersing in a tender Summer gloat.

Reaching my hand into the trench of my pocket,
I remove a small knife

and carve my way to the afternoon blitz of smashing bronze and copper sun.

This Summer day, the preamble of an awaking heart,
softens me to the drench

of tomorrows approaching rain. By evening,
I stiffen my eyes to the chew of the deer,

a fistful of doe clamor to the proud blanket of heavy nightfall.

Donny Barilla

Alive in the Glades

Into the thicket, grotto
lined by the swift wave of the Spruce
and the tremor of the most ancient Sycamore, I-
stepped to the boldest spear. The joust of the onion
stalk which perished beneath my foot.

I reach the clumsy lining
of the mumbling woods, and I-
felt the sun splash against the deepest tans of my
leathery flesh, bold
the pouches in the deep of my mouth,
tickle it's way to the sweat beads
rustling across each bone and crevice of my forehead.

From a slivered look,
the smallest of creeks punch their way
across meadow and bush, leaned against the antiquated oak.
I gather a mouthful of water
as I feel the shards sting with each swallow.

Now, alive in the glades of an eager tomorrow,
slices of battering finches and spry of the fox
whimper at the clamor of my foot, my boot.
I hold the passage of fattening Summer. I quake
to the sultry leaves, carved nuts, and steeped branches
as they wilt beneath the heaviest of suns.

DANCE UPON THE FOREST FLOOR

Country Dreaming

I awoke from a heavy slumber, deep
in the lusty countryside.

A woman approached me.

She asked who I was and why I slept
in the open field.

~

Here are the pouches of my ears-
they are the winds upon the naked ocean, wildly
alive I can hear the osprey.
I can hear the swish of their
swaggering legs.

Keen are the sting of my eyes-
I can see the galaxy make love
on my fingertips. Softly, the stars
drip like trembling sweat beads
down my cheeks.

And my cheek are the sweetest pies
steaming like the fog of morning
as they rest on a counter
so close to the trust of an open window.

Donny Barilla

My fingers tilled the soil of each field, the farmer's
oxen still smells my thumb.
Full breasted women
tug for milk with the crooning cow.

My healthy arms are the rivers
winding and kissing the most fertile drench
of soot and rolling mineral.
My chest are the lakes
as they smooth their way
across the endless groin of the earth.

This, my love, is who I am.

Until the Close of Day

I tread the palm of my hand
with a slight direction upon these patches
of emerald clovers. I sopped so slowly the dew
trembling beneath the earliest of daylight showering upon
both creek and somber close of flowers at Autumn breath.

Removing the pouch of shoe and sock.
I slipped my pale, soft feet through the mumbling
meadow. Eager morning daylight
smashed across the paleness of my face, I-
swallowed the powdery breeze, gingerly turned away.

Donny Barilla

Summer Showers

The once quiet slant of the heaven
slashes into a prism, as I-
fall to the soft Summer grass, moist.

I hear the crows as they slowly surrender
to silence. The wrapping winds struggle
across me. I slumber in this warm cocoon.

Sulking at Nightfall

The sky bloomed to delicate pinks and bled
the color purple. Soft winds slumped
across my face, neck, and torso. From these distant horizons, cliffs
which slung from neighboring mountains. I watched
the hawk scour the landscape, hunting.

Alive, the most paused breeze
kissed me upon both mouth and cheek.
Her spiced perfumes, heavy like musk, towered
across me. I felt this craving for her
and the damp grasses hugged my foot, roamed
across my ankle.

Before nightfall, I sulked as I yearned for the press
of her abdomen and breast.

Soft Smile

I approach her in humid milks
Enter her in the creams of madness
From another room the old woman steeps tea
An hour later we join her and softly smile.

DANCE UPON THE FOREST FLOOR

Hungry Flash

By morning stars vacate the heavens
Fading glimmer of nights fable loosened
Insects climb the farmhouse wall
The sun extemporizes in a hungry flash.

Donny Barilla

Clamor the Ground

The welcoming maple offers shade and silent love
Stretching a gnarled branch and stem
Inside an infant cries, surrendering the long Spring afternoons
In a fragment of a moment maple leaves clamor the ground.

Buzz and Steep

Women glaze themselves in suspense
Silk sheets offer a crisp velvet welcome
Summer night the children play in a neighboring yard
Excitement of the evenings buzz and steep.

Donny Barilla

Nibbling Seeds

The mother reveals her breast to a hungry child
Anticipation stirs from puckering lips
Above the cottage a murder of crows land
Nibbling seeds from an overhanging tree.

Shards and the Crimping Earth

I spoke to the death of the old woods, so slowly
each dash of the falling leaves
scattered across the frozen dirt path
scouring through the ancient forest.

~

With the eager lift of my aching neck, head
I softened to the spread of snowflakes
fumbled in shards upon the crimp of gnarled earth.

Donny Barilla

Down

Along the leaves, emerald green, I traced my fingers
against vein and contour.

Mist washed on the edge of my lips.
Fog pressed its way through the fatness of the thick forest
which spoke to the dripping moisture, spoke of longing.

Heavily, I sat on the closest log.
I watched night descend like a comforter of down.

Moonlit Leaves

Sun drips away,
a shroud of dimness pillows
through the dancing oak leaves.

Moonlight sulks across each brown
wiggling leaf. I walk to the faint glimmer
and host the dead grasses

with the tamp of my boots.

Donny Barilla

Elm Leaves

Through the fist of Autumn, I
spread every finger across the jigsaws of your
dancing muscles which motioned across
your back and shoulders.

Standing by riverside, I saw a piece of driftwood
and thought of you, alive in the crouch of falling leaves.

I fashioned a photo I took of you last Summer
and smiled as the elm leaves floated downstream.

DANCE UPON THE FOREST FLOOR

Fur Trees

The emerald fur trees
sloped across the edge of the flowered meadow
so alive with prowling grasses
and the waving tuft of the onion stalk
which spoke of each mineral of
dirt growing beneath, so rich and vibrant.

I held the smallness of her hand
tucked and folded into mine.

We paused in the thicket of weed and shrub,
I turned to her and slithered my hands
across the nape of her neck.
Softly we kissed.

A gentle wind threshed through the evergreen forest.
I smoothed my gaze to the fumbling
woods and recalled the taste of each fragrance
which swabbed around my face and tossed through
my flickering hair.

Robins

Trimmed along the edge of the home,
two holly bushes filled themselves with berries;
I watched the robins feast in twitches near the deepest green.

She sat beside me and sunk her fingers against my palm, I-
smiled as Autumn breath danced across us,
filling our lungs with crisp sobriety.

The fattest of birds landed at our feet, he took flight,
then vanished through the fogged skyline.

I ran my eyes through the mists of her hair
and kissed her with the humid press of my mouth.

Molecules

Beneath her dress moaned galaxies.
Probing from the ices of her fingers
I shuddered from my back to my legs
which drew forth the most supple ointments
and jams.

Stinging through the space between us,
I glanced at her, eased to the wheat
which drew a hot breeze,
making her hair as full as the leaves clinging to the oak.

The bed drew forth a spasm
as each molecule, both mine and yours,
slithered in sweats from body to mouth.

Donny Barilla

From Orchard to Rolling Stream

Orange, yellow flickering light
strode through the pasture
and trembled across soft leaves
which sulked to the fertile earth-
I spoke to tree and branch.
I tickled each stem and snap of a soft peach haze,
a luster of Autumn breath.

I walk through the calm, quiet orchard.
Icy stalk of the onion root and frozen glaze
of this tender frost, the endless needles
of the nearby gloating pine rests like a crown-
forest prince unravels both sap and eager bark.
Gently, caressing winds nurse the chill
coiled in the bones of my face.

In a calming kneel, I cup the chilled stream water
in the goblet of my hand. The evening moon
fumbles through the sky and all its gentle pastures
as a burgundy stretch of light tickles-
rapids and graze of the trout stream.
I stand loosely watching a slice of driftwood
carry through the dam in soft eddies.

Mountain Spring

Midday. The trees were feverish and alive.
I reach to the trickling mountain spring
and watch the colors of the sun dance
upon each small ripple and gush.

I drank with a heavy swallow.

Leaves trembled across the small path.

Donny Barilla

Her Summit

Across her ivory breasts
I surrendered to a powdery glaze-
asleep, the moon pampered it's way through
the fogged crest of my window.

She shook as I reached her summit.
I fell to the arms of the thickest aroma.
She welcomed me as an altar, heavy
rattling of her trembling torso, legs and bust.

Hyacinth

I stood on the patio, so smooth
the sulking Autumn breeze fell across me.

Lighting a smoke,
gentle leaves danced to my shoulders and chest.

The sky swelled in an open mouth
as the smash of a river's arrival.

Each stroke of wind
flickered through the fine limpness of my hair.

I sat, leaned against the strong wall
where I slumbered and lived.

I look to the horizon
and see purples like the hyacinth
-stretch across the churning sky.

Donny Barilla

Brittle Winter

Fog and mist fell to the frozen ground
as fabric, swabbed from an infant,
tamped upon each snap of grass and weed.

Wrapping the coil of lace and boots, I-
walked the edge of the tree line
feeling the stitch of my iced beard and sting of my cheeks.

Kneeling in a haunch, I cupped a pine cone
chipped and battered. I threw it into the thicket
of frosted woods and heard the spirit of the forest
-moan into the avenues of brittle Winter.

Quaking Breads

Water soothed from the flower
perched to the late Summer sky.

I fell to the trembling thighs.
Breasts alive like quaking breads
sulked through the mild, soft day.

I slept on each surfacing breath, I tamped
my lips against her fruited pulps.

Donny Barilla

Distant Shore

Sleeves pulled, she
leaned and rested her soft cheeks and slightly opened jaw
as the candle flickered to the ceiling
and a tear of wax slipped to the floor.

Pinched with fingers, smoke
kissed the musky draft and spread as a gown
of incense.

I traced my lips across the sweats of her breasts
as I felt the salt water of a distant shore.

Row Boat

Looking from the row boat,
the leagues beneath him tugs with the minerals.

This pond carries the steam
rising as a damp kiss to humid Summer air.

He smiles to her face, slithers from
each lingering scent spooling from her neck.
-the heaviest spice.

Lean, his arms row so slowly, she
cleverly, softly unbuttons her blouse.

The waters mist saunters,
clinging between them.

Donny Barilla

Bundles of Yarn

Bundles of yarn, thickets of thread
rests gently across forests of her lap.
Gently, mosses stretch her hooking toes.

Leaning close, she undoes her stitch,
-unravels a promise.
Warmth surrounds her, moist pads of loose minerals.

Buttons fall to twigs and patches,
alive through the rooted stem,
pale white extends milky colors, slender arms.

I suspend dampened curves of her shoulders.
I scour from breast to breast,
feed until I satiate, full.

-

I knead the thumb and crook of my hand,
rain begins, taps upon the foggy mirror,
dampening, the early buds open as the width of her mouth.

Comforter of Down

The curled yellow, browned leaf
loosened from the eldest tree, as it
fumbled branch and stem through the adjacent treetops.

I stood in a passing sweep, lumbered
and caught the ancient leaf in the cup
of my trembling hands.

Into the calm of the dying woods, I heard
the oak, elm, and spruce moan.

I slipped the sliver of parchment
well into the deep of my jacket pocket.

Softly, I turned my head and witnessed
the forest floor lay as a comforter of down
for the shake of my thickly chilled legs.

April 26, 2016 Pennsylvania Landscape

Crouching, the green grass blades
begged upon the smooth of each bead of trembling water
slid to the mineral soil -quiet dispersion.

Within the hour, a gush of wind lifted
the clinging mist, fog which rubbed against
plump spruce and deepening root.

I gathered the stick in the coarseness of my knuckle and palm, I-
Swallowed the steaming coffee and swiped across the lusty field.

A gleam of sun slapped gently onto the hushing tree branches.
Bloated through the fog with a groan, winds surfed
across the quivering stretch and tossed the crinkled leaf.

Drought

Post by post, retort of the crow,
nurturing the dry soil of an earth
raped by the hateful sun.

Each bird -spotting a dead mouse
scamper with grievance of a still and hungry
absorption of day and thirsty beak.

The small girl dances by yellow tufts of grass,
ordered to chisel the remembrance of summers suffering.
The grandfather smiles and looks away.

The creek, a few hundred miles away,
smells of dried mud,
sluicing in threads of watery minuets.

The meadow has never been a meeting place,
a place where women pluck their water,
and admire another woman's husband.

By nightfall, youth from
farm and stacking hay,
The girls kiss their boys thirsty lips.

Donny Barilla

Apple Grove

By apple grove, the pond lurked a fine green film
as I swelled my breath through the ciders which bloomed through the air.

Snapping the stem of this red breasted fruit, I-
crunched the skin and dug swiftly into the flesh.

In a gentle turn, I sat by pond's edge
and roamed my eyes through the velvet fleece

filtering across this plump, gravy water.

By morning, I awoke and trekked to the distant hills
which curved as the waist of each woman, each bed of starving evergreen.

Smooth Water

She lay beneath me as a
creek beneath a blanket of wool.

Swiftly, I gather her, saps from the maple, robust, strong.
From her mouth seeped the morning glisten.

I sweetly touch from navel to fleshy films,
slow drippings, she bound to me

in pastures of my drifting waters,
on the moss and fern, she waded, gently came to me.

Pebbles fell about us in rhythms,
gathered to the chill of a neighboring creek.

I placed a soft kiss upon her,
the red spruce showered to the waterway.
Spun in eddies, small circles, in a moment
tangled with the dam of fractured sticks, mud packed and heavy,

yet lightly grabbed by the wooded curving bend,
I waded steeply across the murky bed, surrounded by smooth water.

Donny Barilla

California Gold

Reaching my hand, both thumb and nook,
the oranges nestled in my palm, I-
felt the beaches of California
blast their gold as the thud
of my tongue wilted a slippery juice-
Seeping syrups permeate the corners
of my eager lips.

I wrestled her from her sweatpants
and cotton t-shirt.

Lashing in the sulk of a nearby pounding windowpane-
we dipped into the marvel of heavy morning.

Sparrows rest on my ledge,
murmuring a choral triumph.
Seeds fall to the ferns, wavering
patched mosses and the ancient tree.

We met in the smoothest of arrivals.

From the Tender Current

I brought the icy milks from the tender current of the creek
and drank in the murmuring ripples
through the mist and falling fog.
I spoke of softness and lusty waves
which roamed across my forearm and hands.

Gently, the sky opened.
I took her in my arms-
coiled her as thread across
the thunder of her moaning voice as sweat
trickled about me.

She slithered through the fat of the pasture
and tickled the grassy tufts and fed the close by patch of mint.

FALLEN BLOUSE...

Blouse and Gown

Your voice rambled like a tea kettle.
I soaked in your verbs, tender upon my ear.

Soft salted beads wiggled upon the perch
of my mouth, gentle syrups, tang on my tooth and gum.

We lulled through the quivers of nightfall.
Forever, I will recall the dampness of your thighs.

Tenderly, the silks of your walnut colored hair
still roam the crests and peaks of my torso,
slept upon like a canvas.

I wrestle the nook of your chilled fingers and thumbs.
I glance outside and watch as the leaves fall to the ground
-a slight undressing of blouse and gown.

Alone at Midnight

Her dress slipped to the cold wooden floor
as I watched her lips come to me in
a drift like a ghost as her breasts
motioned to me- a burning temple.

The coffee mug trembled.
I felt the sap of her mouth
riddle across me in honeys and nectar.
She spoke in vapor, quietly her fingers combed my hair.

I felt the meat of her waist
thicken across me as the room rattled,
sauces of her eyes showered the floor.
She was a burst of citrus upon my naked chest.

By morning, I coiled in the oldest of linens,
I churned through the swollen room.

DANCE UPON THE FOREST FLOOR

Dreaming in Autumn

I loosened her garments.
Leaning forward to the window, she showered
in the fabrics of the Autumn sun.

Maples shred each leaf
and quivered the loss of sapling and buds.

Softly, I placed my lips on the nape of her neck
and gently her fragrant scents stretched across
the bed, sheets, and pillows of down.

She livened the emerald moss as we walked
deep into the thick of the woods
which bathed us in mint and humble jasper.

Paused, we lay on the carpeting of leaves, reds and browns.
I fell upon her in the creams and milks
which fell on the ripe fruits of thigh and abdomen.

~

I awoke to the scents of coffee.
The window rattled as the moaning sky.
Fog dripped in grays and fallen beads.

Donny Barilla

Full Moon Naked

The fullest moon undressed itself,
nude as the thin clouds spread away-
a spirited breast with crown and soft gloat
vapors streamed from my lips
nights robes stretched into distant powders.

Evergreen

The sun flickered in golds, smashing
across the waves stretching in ripples and watery tugs.

As I sat so softly by the riverbank
I watched as the mourning dove sulked

through the trembling air, alive
with the scent of the grooming waters

which grew rich in minerals and coat of the nearest rock
swabbed in kelp and stroking soot.

I knelt, drank the chill from the icy water.
In the flash of the sky which dwelt behind the fat of the sun,

I slumbered with the mouths of each rippling wave
tugging at the yearning pulse of my tender feet.

I stood as the sky opened it's dam and stooped
beneath the quiet evergreen.

Donny Barilla

Stooped to the Lilac Bush

The sky was a cotton shroud of thin grays
and ribbons of the glancing moon.

I walked through the yard and felt the velvet
jade colored grass stretch around my hooking toes.

I stooped to the lilac bush. I smiled.
Dew droplets gleamed upon each flickering leaf

which cupped as a endless ocean cove
aware of salts and white rippling waves.

A thin patch of grass and a neighboring crouch
of slender onion sprouts fondled the rushing winds.

I turned, faced the gushing scents of mint,
sweetly the pressing gusts from the north swabbed across
my limbs and wavering silky hair.

Straight into the thick of night
I wade through blades of green and pausing dew.

Daybreak

The sky peels from blue, navy canvas,
landing, sweet rains gather a silky minuet of pond, small creek.

Swiftly, hands rub the crisp, lathering bedside
where puddle and water holes
touch upon my tongue and mouth.

I can see the early squirrel, tempt of the chipmunk, flesh torn
shriek of the morning hawk, fast with piercing eyes.

In a swift movement and turn of my torso and bust,
the angry fish shatters the stillness of the meandering stream.

I walk a mile, then a mile more, the crows take flight
and dart to the billowing
tuft of winds from the early hours of daybreak.

Donny Barilla

Cape Cod

Winds off the ocean's skin
flickers across your ebbing waves, shaking breasts.
I taste your salts on the tip of my tongue
and breath to the distant buoy and glamor of each lighthouse
marking a remembrance where we touch.

In the brightness of morning, I rest on the puckering sands
and watch the fisherman thrash their
chilled legs and feet. The fish argue about the nights madness
which washes to the shore in a flash.
Kelp stretches and yearns for the foot and calf of the fisher.

I return to the small cape cod
swabbed with trickling pearl beads, water beads.
Sitting on the soft down of the bed, I kiss
the sandy grit of her lips and caress the malts of her thighs
swimming to the distant coves where she dreams.

Squall

Light blitzed like a vein
between the darting gray clouds.

Fresh rain pasted to my fine, limp hair-
my eyes witnessed

geese routing through skies edge>
courting in a perfect V.

Shaking indoors, I light a damp smoke,
breathed the charcoal vapors

as the film crawls to the top of the dresser
and ceiling.

Light softly returns.
I hears the song of the probing robins.

Shoreline

Sand grabs at feet,
crisp waves texture both ankle and foot,
-slice of the horizon.

Birds fleck in ribbons,
bloodied clouds moan of coming night,
in all it's regal entropy, promise.

Weeks later,
I reenter the sandy gown,
lush carpets of all curving bends and retreat.

Tiny stones
sketch the heavy
shoreline.

Gilded Rays

In the slant of the glinted rays,
gray cottons of passing clouds,
I gather the gilded smash of sun
which ordains to the Autumn sky.

I boast of a passing haze of dust and
flickering golds hush the grasses
of each meadow, spreading across
the velvets of a quiet earth.

I hold dominion of this place
as do you.

I share in every breath.
Cupping the glaze of your
palm, the crunching frost
grows as a skin, film across
-the groin of the earth.

Donny Barilla

Lovemaking in the Winter Hour

Her hands-like icicles
slipped beneath my belt
and buckle. Weaved through the foliage
of my chest and groin.

Her lips- painted a deep crimson
tugged warmth from beneath
my skin, my tender thighs.
I felt the heat pound against the freeze
of my abdomen and I crept to the surface
of her tongue, so softly I breathed.

I am witness to the crescent curve
of her doughy breasts.
I sank, deepened into her
tepid and alive- her snow powdered skin.

Together we melted
and sulked, reborn into a genuflect
of pulsing hot veins, drip of the fragrant bush.
I reached inside of her
and mumbled a verb of enticement-
plasmas flush across in winters breadth.

At the Machias

I dipped, swam through the icy arms
of the heavy Machias.
I heard the tears of the slithering grass
fall as a glisten- a dying frost.

In the gloat of the visible distance
I heard a scream, from tumbling pastures
there was a fall across the slap of the ocean.
I turned my head, bust and welcomed the winds
as they tunneled above the calmness -
the saps of the bushes begged for touch.

I heard the cry of the black fly, as it steeped
through the buckling winds.
I softly screamed to the roof of the fog dipped earth.
Sweetly, I love the fly as it dreamed it's way
to the Machias- slow I surrender.

I could feel the slippery dew of morning.
I feel the throb of the Autumn.
A glaze to forested floor, a thin gauze,
I revealed myself to the sauce of cove and bend.

Donny Barilla

Pit and Pail

The plums withered in the sun
-withered with age. I smell the sweetness
rising to the palate of the careful breeze.

I bent and gathered a few in my palm.
My teeth snapped the naked black flesh
and hurriedly it seeped across my lips,
corners of my mouth, which opened
like a draw bridge and slapped my
tongue and fumbled to the back of my
throat.

The stem of my plums yearned for
the tree and it's fathering roots.
I can feel the flesh of the plum, sap
across the pit and pail of my chest, stomach.

I dug a generous hole in the earth,
I buried the raped pit, waiting for a good rain.

Summer Heat

With lightning dashing from the joust of my tongue
I swam into her, the inks of the sky, spread poison

through both vein and an endless cavern of life. I swept,
circling dust above the crest of my torso and bust.

The porch held the hand of the mashing rains. I-
witness to the flickering lights, held by the backdrop

of nightfall, each felt rivulet dresses the dust
into a smolder of soft buzzing light. I could hear

country music dazzle the late night which conference
the jazzes of the tumultuous dust. Calmly, I-

gathered the hot flesh, as if born of the apple,
a crack, snapping bite from her skin. Juice, plasma, and

tepid creams positioned from her valleys where her
meadows begged, nursed the grimace of the sky.

I recall her allowing the dress she wore falling-
caressing the curve of the gentle dresser and bed.

Donny Barilla

I submitted to the slippery touch of finger, thumb, and cuticle.
I pressed into her and I felt the sprinting static and loosen,

the deepening charge wilts around me. The fire of the night sky
fumbles around me as I whimper in all subtlety.

Belly Dancer

She spread herself in oils, butters.
Like a snake she danced,
movements flickered, a candle stretched to the ceiling.
A passage of silent verbs quaking to the music,
quivering belly and breasts which glanced to nectar,
feet tug the silent floor, clutched walls,
slithering hands through juices crimped in adoration.

The mussels quaked for some time,
soft against the moist tongue.
He shot his thumb to his finger
-and swallowed.
A stiffness fed the hungry mouth,
his stomach became a cavern.
Swiftly, she ran her fingertips
smoothly across his face and smiled.

Donny Barilla

Scribbles from Hera's Diary

Children who swim in the mouth
of endless islands, jaunt me with the venom
of my tired breast.

I coil to the lightning which still
throbs in the pouch of my thighs
and I murmur the breath of my sweet sons and sweet daughters.

To the humming sounds
of the perfect lyre which glitters
beneath a troubled sun, dances through the tepid air.

Children fracture the glaze of a weary earth.
I gently watch the chase and I smile upon the capture
where she melds upon both river and sea.

Clusters of forbidden fruit tingle upon my tongue.
I slumber, dream of the world when fluids reigned.
Quietly, I kneel to the smack of a tireless bolt.

Zeus' Thunderbolts

Glittering smash on the inked black skyline
tampers and clutters in a feverish web.

A heavy spoken rush and roar
slash upon the nearby ocean, spread in a satchel of waves.

The blues of deep night
harbor the nestling verbs of fury,

nearby, the fishing boat, swamped upon an enticed island
crimps to the fading passages of approaching rains.

Heavy electric bolts splint the helpless tree
where the anchored clipper breathes in maddening fear.

The small birds, seemingly disappear,
the coconuts roll for a tousle or two,

the mossy gravel and fern
usher the temptation of windy reach.

AS ONE PONDERS THE QUIET THAW

Thaw

Crisp, the smooth gems of rain fell upon my withered skin,
each splash dampened in bursting galaxies,
calm my freckled and patterned flesh.

Leaned back, my mouth agape, I could taste the nebula
dance across my tongue. I thought of you in the sliver
of a second, then, faded to the dripping dark.

Rising to the press of early Spring, I felt, smelled
the roaming mulch as it pampered each pore
and sulked with each wavering bed of ferns.

Sour sticks from the deep of last Winter
gathered in the death of broken brotherhood.
I carved my way past and searched for the heaviest
of early bloom.

The pants, boots, and dampest flannel
spoke of the gushing rain.

Finding the forest bed, scattered as a puzzle,
I sipped the pooling creek, chiseled in the melt
of chipped ice and I danced to the flicker of warming rain.

Donny Barilla

I moved to the gait of the surmounting rains.
Quietly, the earth moaned as I gathered a few stones
buried last Fall. I wander the breast of the woods.

I am alive in the thick creams and quivering buds
of this hungry bloom.

Undressing

To her, I opened the edge of my morning eyes.
I saw the brown hazelnut sink so deep
into the crest upon her cheeks.

Touching the cool trickle of her icy hands, I shook
to the pirouettes as they slide across my chest and neck.

Her mouth was a furnace slithering steam.
From her tongue, oils dripped forth upon me.

From abdomen to the fields of wheat
roaming between her thighs, I could smell
the earth come to life.

Reached, I smoothed my hands against the fleshy
skins of her waist and tapped my thumbs across
with silent rebuttal in the freeze of frosted morning.

Into the snapping winds of morning, I silently
listened to windows smack and I heard the crackle
of mingling branches as they danced amidst a gushing breeze.

Quietly, I listened to the sobs of Winter undress.

From the Grave

I slouch beneath the slithering sun.
She sheds the dampness of the showering sky
and looks upon me, so inviting.

I turn from this birch wood.
Eager, I hear the moans of my groin.
Chipped, the white bark sulks upon the ground.

The cry of the mushroom, patterned in spots,
giggles upon the roaming wind.

This earth bed dreams beneath my feet
and I hear it's quaking tremors, soft the grave.

DANCE UPON THE FOREST FLOOR

Waiting for Warmth

In February, the meadow boasted of it's nudity.
The remains of slowly dripping icicles swaggered
and hung from the heavy oak as each branch
wilted upon the breath of a warming sky.

~

By the patch of gloating trees, the earth soaked
with black soil and peppered white minerals.

In the distance, I heard the crows shred their ink black
wings and carry the breeze beneath the feathers.

~

By the water well, I flicked a coin to the deep.

Pouches of snow roamed the edge.

So long I thirst for this meadow to climb to life.

I shut my eyes and witness her arms open to the wandering notes
of a tender sun.

Shades of Green

Dampness thickened throughout the air, climbing
moisture yet settling upon the grassy spread.

Weeds and ancient mulch, soaked from last year,
unleashed a yawning thirst.

~

The nave of the stream, coiled in a sapped and slippery
bedded cove hosted each pebble and jagged rock
as I tossed them to the their origin, the threading waters.

When the wind surmounted mints, I
paused and smiled as the trembling breeze fumbled
upon my ash gray beard.

~

Following the curve of the creek, I stood close to the evergreen,
the spruce, and pine.

I smiled as the trees shook their shades of green.
A gathering of pine needles grew so inviting.
I lay softly and slept.

By Lakeside

Winds slope across my face and dancing flannel.
Swiftly, I embrace the arms of a deafened January, which
groans through the death of tree branches and speaks
with the crinkling parchments of every fallen leaf.

~

I gently open my mouth and gather
the sobbing trickle of the falling snow.

The lake was a brick of ice.
I stood on frozen waters edge and watched
the oldest oak leaf scurry across surface,
then stick so snug to rock and rotting log.

~

By evening, pinks bleed to purples
and the Winter fattens for a heavy birth.

I lean as a trellis against each coughing tree.
The limbs and twigs flutter and groom
with powdery white.

Donny Barilla

Scent of Autumn

Scampering across the leafy earth,
the tan breasted bird snatched a seed.

I stood by and watched the twigs roll
in the rippling waves, a high crest of capped waves.

Suddenly, the soft, cool wind dredged.
I could taste the flavors of Autumn

which quicken at my face and burning ears.

~

Looking upon the kneeling clouds
sunk from the passing skyline, I stood

and witnessed the cabins stand like sentinels of lakes edge
guarding the soft dome and sulking

against the maze of the patterned forest.

~

DANCE UPON THE FOREST FLOOR

Here, the giggling leaves, so robust,
drifted across the chilled icy water.

Hearing her voice,
the smoothest of words tendered across the volleying winds.

I sank my teeth to the saucy flesh of Autumn,
disrobing upon the dredge of the crackling branches,
these foams and froths sank to the carpets of gathered leaves.

Milk

The rain sliced through the sky.
Leaves cupped, gathered the tender juice
pocketed in the upturned veins.

Within the farmhouse, the young mother
removed her breast.

Puckering the pulps during the dance
of this Summers breach and fracture,
the crimp of the infant sulked in this treasure.

~

Morning. She plucked the basil, thyme.

Mud gathered about her ankle and heel.
Sauces hung to the sliver of each grass blade.

Sipping a ceramic mug of bristling coffee, she
found a walnut, caked in the clays of a forgotten earth.

Stirring within her, she felt her milks stir.

Winter Blooms

The earth froze as a tomb.
Clay, cracked rock, and quilts the shade of white
met with the slow dripping fogs
lining the naked bush and patched mosses.

Alone. Starved. The crow winced upon the muddled and vast thinning air.
Words crooned upon the grazing wind.
Snap of the branch and quiet cultivations
dredged this Winter breeze.

In a gentle pause, I heard
the screaming sky descend among us-
from withered leaves to the sulking log, trunk.

Peering to the distant mountains, I
watched the slabs of ice.

Mists and dripping skies blanket,
I can see each particle of these insurmountable
blanched jagged boulders. I weep for a moment-
then continue.

Donny Barilla

At End of Day

I stood silent as the deepest breath of Winter gushed across me.

They came from gnarled bushes and sodden hills.

At the dam, the slapping river gave way.

They came from this gathering of stones, words.

I felt the ices frock to the flesh upon my cheeks and neck.

They came slow, so very slow.

As I opened my frigid mouth, snowy flakes drizzled on my tongue.

Alive, they touched my skin and I clenched my fist with a burn.

Dead, the weeds crinkled against my shoe.

I heard the moans of the fattening sky which fell like a blouse at nightfall.

Sweet blood seeped through my lips and I spoke slowly.

They roamed forever across the earth and smiled to the purple horizon.

I smiled at the glaze of this satin finish.

DANCE UPON THE FOREST FLOOR

Swooned in Early Spring

I came to her along the thickest jaunt of woods.
For her, I begged the sweet dove to 'coo'.

Upon an endless spread of tree and trunk, I
wished for the bareness of her breasts.

Slight, the chill of this damp early Spring, I thought
of her and the fall of the sulking blouse, deep reds and tans.

Embraced upon the quick breathing winds,
she promised warmth, food upon my tongue.

As I stood by the slithering stream, the channel
softly came to life, scents of the earth engaged in it's thaw.

The clever bush and moan of the crocus lulled
me to a flickering grip of blossom and bud.

~

By end of day, I sobbed. By the smoothness of night
I clung to the rubbing climes of moonbeams, so tender.

Donny Barilla

She hid beneath the shrugging silks of the moist soil.
I slept in the pale swab of her arms.

Her flickering eyes lulled through the black blanket of night.
I fell to the gesturing wash of these hands, so soft.

As the Fog Fades

Feeling the pulse of nights breath,
sweet, the lilacs loaf over my body, sulk
to the scents foundering about my gray beard and face.

I can see her deep in the pollens and meadow.
Sauntering to the breath of the falling clouds,
I walk among the silky mists.

~

Damp, my eyes awoke in the fattening brisk showers
where morning spritzes rose water.

Midday, I gloat to the sun.
She fades to the nearest trim of forest.
Her soft words fade as the fog begins to lift.

Donny Barilla

Taking Time

I shy my way from the cruel, white snow
alive in all it's powders and daring ice.

By Spring, the Wintery mesh will turn
to porridge. The glancing sun grooms
each thread of wheat.

I speak to each tree as I pass. In reply,
I listen to the bark and branches moan.

~

By thick strokes of the chipped pond,
alive in the passages of tossing cool water,
I pause, look for a long time.

Mother Winter declares.

I walk the edge of the thinning forest.
I stumble upon the birth of a great slouching mountain.
I walk a few miles, then pause again.

Searching the Pines

The fog drifted, waves of a forgotten sea.
I paused about the pine tree,
soaked in the bite of each needle, ripening saps.

Wilted, the cones fell,
Icarus upon the rocky floor.

I stood and walked my way.
With a white glaze upon the grassy bed,
I heard, felt the snap and crunch
of the persuasive charging Spring.

I walked to the crest of this mulching hill.
Life, for the first time this year,
shed it's drafty fragrance.

Stopping for a moment, spreads
of moss draped across the tree, scattered rocks.

The tree, this monument, carved
through the caked crust of the hardest earth,
stood proud among the breath of gust and wind.

Leaning upon the trunk, I swam in the chill
of the earliest Spring.

Donny Barilla

Wooded Silence

Woods crackled through swift winds.
Then, silent.
After a generous moment, I heard an acorn
fit tight in the piled leaves.

I looked to the blue satin sky.
Thin spreads of cotton clouds
swept upon the treetops.

Then again, all fell silent.
Looking through the sparse, somber woods,
-geese ventured south.

Breakfast

Sleeves cluttered about the smooth slope of her arms.
As she brought me a warm cup of coffee,
a fragrance from her hair swept over me.

My eyes softened to the print of her long,
gripping t-shirt which curved around her hips and thighs.

~

The pounding winds smacked the kitchen window.
I heard the click of a closing refrigerator door.

Her kisses purred about my ears and my eyes softened upon
each pale cream of her breasts.

~

I stood. Looking out the cracked window,
I watched the gnarled branch and ancient tree.

Glancing back, she opened the wheat of her field.
Taking a moment, I slithered upon her.

Fantasy, Pennsylvania 2017

With slippers, molding the early Spring grass,
joust of the wind surfaces across me.

Tender sway of the bamboo shoots
clip their way to the cream colored clouds.

The driveway, chipped with pebble and stone,
hosted a dancing tuft of rising weeds.

Slumped in the lawn chair, clever ants spooled
around my feet, digging deeply into the earth.

Running my thick fingers through my beard, I
recall the frost of a season passed.

~

Later, I stood by the spindling, stretching creek.

Glancing upon the threading water, I threw a stone which skipped

then reach the crackled, hard mud upon the other side.

The nearby cherry tree drizzled blossoms.

DANCE UPON THE FOREST FLOOR

I watched with loose eyes. The dancing petals curled through rapids

as I felt the breeze groom upon my neck.

~

Shifting my gaze, I heard the gasp of the heavy oak tree.
I smiled, then, roamed for a while.

Pocketing an acorn, the rain slapped and pattered.

Donny Barilla

Robes of Spring

The breeze fell upon us,
wrapped us in spools,
fed us the moist droplets from the tender
leaf and and crimping cup of the very same leaf.

Looking skyward,
the rain slapped us upon the face
and we leaned back and sopped our
starving throats.

~

I look to the thin haze of the skyline.

Grays and ash colored clouds trembled.

We felt the paste of our hair

glisten upon our scalp.

I turned to her and softly we kissed.

~

DANCE UPON THE FOREST FLOOR

Mud grew tender about our feet.
The ink black crows took flight as we
embraced the scented mulch
which opened as a well patterned dress.

Into the stretch of day,
into the stretch of night,
we tamped through the clever robes of dancing Spring.

Donny Barilla

Autumn Compromise

I rest by the sacred sycamore.
Leaves collect by my feet, legs.
Looking to the thin gauze of the sky,
I think of her,
slowly I place my cheek upon her breast.
I feed well into the hush of Winter.

Remembering Youth

The sky stretched as marble columns.

Into the wet grassy deep, I fell upon the riverbank

where we touched as children, suspended above ourselves

and withering of thirst.

I gave her the ointments of my youth.

From the weary distance, I heard the crows

wrestle forth with 'caw' and eager screech.

As in these memories, the sky still hung gray.

I could taste the milks of her breasts as they never were before.

The crocuses flushed and spread the sweet pollens

gripping upon a drift, I stood so still, the river dust

pasted the color yellow.

Donny Barilla

Onto the path, leading home, I felt the retreat of groin

and the wilting palms of my hands.

Clammed shut and gnarled as the drifting tree branch

I wept for her absence, distant stream, sky.

The Fountain

The coin slipped through the silk water,
slithered to the granite basin, bottom
where silent voices still murmured.

~

I sat for a distance, a journey.
I waited for the song to begin.
I faded within the wrapped warmth of my jacket.

~

Heavy breath fell upon my ears
and the sting of my reddened cheeks.

Her lips were full as blossoms
dancing into the breath of Springs nudity.

~

We met here. Soaked in the treasures of heat and white sun.
Trimming my way to the sulk

of her heavy breasts. I heard a moan of trickling water.
I spoke so soft to the flickering light.

Evening Roams

On the oldest of wooden porches
I sat on the wicker chair.

The fat of the sky bloomed
as the deepest blue hues fed the slender horizon.

Softly, a wild breeze tempered my thinning hair.
I spoke to the girth of moon, alive withing it's circles.

Tugged into the grip of the evening,
I spoke so loudly, the air around us fractured.

I sat silent and softly quiet.
A gentle rain tickled the grassy earth.

The steam from the tea rose as the foggy
mist of nights charm.

I fell upon the slouch of the envious sofa.
I grew damp by the press of misty night.

Forever Lost

The cove slipped across the throat of the earth.
Water softened and smiled in all chilled seduction.

Into the deep of the proud roaming forest
the glade threw pollen and blossoms.

I dug my hooking toes into the grit and mineral
rich earth. My fingers spread as the vein filled oak leaf.

The boldness of her naked chest and abdomen
whispered words of pleasure and Winter's thaw.

I entered the breeze sweeping upon the wheat
fields, edged by thistle and the onion sprout.

Sultry, the mountains enticed. I lift my aching
head and wooed words of Kings and Queens.

I spoke to the endless walls from the endless city gates.
I looked to the rubble and the ancient dust.

She slithered past me again, speaking of home.
I took glance then walked forever.

Donny Barilla

Oceans Foams

The oceans foam slipped across the sands
as an evangelist seeking silks and heavy frocks.

The sky bent, sulked.
I felt the wind rake against me.

Hushing breeze, I met the grainy breath
of the oceans mouth glance through hair, flickering.

Into the most tender moment,
I sent mists of sandalwood and myrrh.

Here, the salted breath of arousal, drew the sweetest
saps and pulled upon the syrups

which roared from coast to the other coast
and sauced upon the horizon.

Her breasts slouched as a temple.
The softness of her eyes glimmered as the nearby
lighthouse, wincing it's way.

DANCE UPON THE FOREST FLOOR

Morning Walk

Shallow water rested upon the narrow trail.
Clays and mud clung to the fading tread on my boots.

Trembling skies threw a silk mist
against the powdery treeline- soft with fog.

Skies opened with a morning blaze, orange and pink.
I fumbled through this mouth, early.

Quivering leaves, shook as the craft of a belly dancer.
Sap and oils dripped from each cupping leaf.

In a moment, the sky slipped about in moisture and syrups.
Quiet, the trail bled from valley to mount.

Donny Barilla

Shadows

The gentle fragrance, from powder to dancing pollen, swept
upon the trembling leaves about the garden
so dearly alive in each mineral of my mind.

She clung as the robust flavors
sapped onto the valleys of my chest.

I dampened against the grains of her mouth,
tenderly dripping in the moistest syrups.

Heavy, her breasts lay soothingly upon the map
of my eager torso.
I softened, slipped as the fires
of the deepest showering shadow of night.

Early Summer

Grasses and thistle, crimping in the tans of an early Summer,
I spoke upon the wind.

Wind flushed and threaded through the glaze
of this pampering breath called life.

Heavy ointments of the dewy beads flashed across
each stretch of sprout and jaunt of onion grass,

while the seething, smooth drip of Summer
doused each blade and soothed each root.

~

The sky grew damp.

I whispered to the hush of warm days, long days.

I thickened my fingers and thumb to the groin of the earth.

Every pausing seed nestled into fibers and grain.

~

I douse upon the breath of Summers crust and dusty fleece.

Donny Barilla

Februaries

Cracked, the asphalt hosted each slush and chip of ice.
Patterned crows danced through the street,
veered for the frozen maple, elm.

The sky swelled in thick marbles
doming across the sky,
spread about with thinned gauze which trembled at the winds.

Nearby, the forest was empty and sopped
with sludge probing the roadside.
I yawned, cupped my hand and withered a humid breath.

~

Trucks, clouted with black fumes,
I stepped aside and ran my fingers through my beard.

~

The walk to the house slapped and crimped my feet,
ankles. I stayed stitched to the warm lining of this
canvased, heavy coat.

~

DANCE UPON THE FOREST FLOOR

Above, the slender trim of the skyline, there broke free
a prism of light.

I rested to the roads gate. Laughing with the crows,
I filled my belly with desire.

Donny Barilla

Threads of Autumn

The oak tree, gnarled and brash
spoke of the soft crinkled leaves which
pampered the ground and grassy hill.

I awoke to the fragrance of Autumn.
Coats of burlap and scents burrowing of sandalwood.

Robins, cardinals doused through the air.
I heard the distant laughter of the wind.

The most remote of the snowflakes
slipped across the rash of the charcoal sky.

Opening the weathered stone from it's burrowing bed, I
placed it in my hands, threw it to the slicing creek.

Looking upward, I witnessed the thinning threads of the open sky.

Pastures gloated as I returned.

TOKENS ON A GIVEN SEASON

Lost in the Open

The sky chose the color apricot.
By midday, clouds dripped in pinks and indigo.

The skyline opened as a vessel,
disrobed the silky thin cottons which stretched.

Lost in the permeating sun,
each beams of light draped across the meadow.

Walking into the thicket,
I felt the starving bush and dance of the pollens.

Paused, the great towering pine tree shed it's burden
upon the bedded, needled forest carpet.

I rested there for an hour and yawned,
I awoke the slow speech of the sappy wood.

~

Removing a photo of my sweet,
I stood and wandered my way home.

Donny Barilla

Siren

The bed sheet opened as an oceans cove,
rattling against the craggy rocks.

I slept upon the softest linens.
I could hear the white capped waves tangle
with each foam and rippling crevice

where salty air dampened through my hair.

She sang of sweet verbs and sweet berries
she would feed upon each who wander the shoreline.

She would unburden the white powders upon her breasts.
Gnarled, her teeth would gnash and bite
as the sailor, hiker, and peasant would pass.

Waves of the great Aegean sea
slithered across the satin, velveteen finish
of a frightened sandy finish.

I was the bones of the dead roaming beach.
Blanched, bleached under the scouring sun.

By nightfall, the mouths of the undressing cove,
nipped upon the tepid water, spoke of flesh and haste.

Forest Floor

Mosses clung and lay as the smallest pastures,
quiet felt bedding and nestling.

She spoke of the low rustling breeze
which tumbled through the leafy trees

and tossed each garment of maple and elm
across the eager quiet forest floor.

~

I replied and said, "open your mouth
and dance with the flicker of your woodlands tongue

which draws sauces from the plants and bushes living nearby.
I open the buttons and stitches of my chest

which pull the drifting heat and snap each passing
chill, turned into a warming draft."

~

She looked at me with regularity.
The gentle wind kissed me upon the lips

as I knelt to the forest floor.

Donny Barilla

Edging the Stream

I turned my bust to the trellised winds
which cornered about each angle of my face, shoulders.

The snapping hook of branch and fumbling twig
scattered upon the leafy ground.

I spoke to the jaunting breeze which lofted
about each forested corner and spread.

Yearning to the face of the north, I slumped
by moss and ran my fingers through each green mumbling fern.

The dancing light through the dancing leaves
reach the brim of my chaffing lips.

~

After a moment, I paused at the green flushing river.

Softly, I watched he minnows swim from edge to edge.

With the snap and parch, I swallowed quick.

DANCE UPON THE FOREST FLOOR

I saw her in the sun.

She bleached her way through the threads of my hair.

So tender, I felt her soften her painted, brightest lips upon my lips.

By nightfall, I slumbered in the darkness of her arms.

Donny Barilla

Summer Love

Her breath slithered as a satin sheet
roaming across the crests of my lips, neck, and abdomen.

Her mouth opened as the pulp of an apple,
snapping skins which awoke to the pressing
jaunt of her icy fingers.

I lay the hot press of her cheeks
upon my trembling mouth.

Every slap of each citrus of each blooming orchard
flaunted in the gems of her eyes.

With the flare of her clavicle and eager breasts,
I molded to the dance of the sun.

DANCE UPON THE FOREST FLOOR

Sleeping with Jasper

Stretching to the star cluttered night,
the oak showered the grassy earth in crumbling leaves.

Leaning, I offered my eyes to the flickering twigs.
With patience, the crisp dancing breeze fell upon me.

~

I slumbered each stitch of crooning nightfall as the gingers
and embedded jasper burrowed around me.

Donny Barilla

Woodlands Come Alive

Winds carried the fibers across the pine scented forest treetops.

Peering upon each branch which swept as a staff,

I could smell the oily sap which moved so slow across the seasons.

In a hurried flash, I looked to the sky and saw peppered fog

and threshing clouds roam through each other.

Pinching with the tips and thumb of my hand,

each emerald bud spoke of the blooming bush,

both lavender and genuflect of the lilac.

I stood deeply within the woods and watched the petals take flight.

Slightly and softly, the petals swirled through the current

of both creek and pond.

DANCE UPON THE FOREST FLOOR

I walked the forest edge.

The sky soothed in purples and lusty pinks.

I made my journey to the meadow and pasture where thistle

and thorn bushes prey upon boot lace and denim.

The oak tree whispered in tongues as I listened closely.

Wind crimped across my old face as I smiled and
looked to each fallen leaf,

engulfed to the dance of the acorn.

So tenderly I smiled.

Donny Barilla

Flesh upon the Ocean

Toes hooked into the flesh of both satin and silky spread.
Knocking breezes slapped at windows and eaves
proud of the dripping rain.

Her dress opened as a cove,
waves danced through the powdered white
of both current and slithering foams
trickling across the beach.

My hands, cupped as a pouch, held the softness
of her breasts.

Dredging their way, each finger, motioned as a minuet.
I spoke to the softness of her abdomen.
Moans gave a thrashing reply.

Into the fattening night,
I drifted upon the valleys which loafed
from nape to nave.

Her flesh crooned as the pillow of down.
I loosened into the drips of cultivating heat.

Roses in the Morning Fog

Petals stroked across the fence.
I watched the sun dance against the stem.
I heard the roots dig into the earth as the morning
fogs arrival moistened in precision and the wind breathed in tempo.

Thorns hooked their way,
guarding as a sentinel.

Every delicate bud stood bold and nude
as the fog lifted, quietly disrobing.

Moisture of the gentle earth, I pulled spices and scents
which caressed about my face.
Together, we moved gently,
fumbling in the palms of my hands and holding tightly
in the lips of my mouth.

Donny Barilla

Awake with Her at Summer's Edge

She sweat, slick and oily as ointments and butters.
Glancing across her shoulders, I could hear

the thrashing leaves of each plant and woodland bush.

Plucking a mint leaf, I sauntered home.

Nocturne in a Dream

Water threading its way down the river—
drew breath and moaned as an instrument.

Heavy and thick branches tuned their way
to the strings of the grassy meadow.

I heard each crackle as the maple loosened
and struck the forest floor.

~

Quick roaming clouds hummed as a symphony.

I threw the pebbles and stones which sank as fugues and preludes.

Ponds of the valley lifted the flooded kelp;

dipping my feet, I softened as the moistest rhythms.

~

Alone, the buried nut sang.
I could hear the growing root
as soil puckered to lip and tongue.

Time Spent with Blackbirds

Sculpting its way across the coiling felts of the pasture,
the fence hosted the stoop of the blackbird.

Today, their song drew no breath as it stayed silent.

Passing trucks along the dirt trail, tan clouds of blooming
powders took a moment to recapture the ground.

I watched as the apricot sun threaded through the trees.

Soon nightfall, I stood and felt the prisms of evening
blanch my face in color.

Standing by thicket and white chipped paints,
I felt the wood splinter against my back.

In the dash of a moment, a breeze patted the coarseness
of my face and old skin.

Ahead, I see the pickup truck pound the dirt
as a blackbird slings into flight.

Beatitudes of a Sacred Earth

I spoke to the clay of the Earth
which pressed against the groin of each scattered leaf.

I gathered the coolest water in my palm
which anointed me with oil and flickering dewdrops.

The caress of the crevice where rock and mud
hosted their display awakened me in their song.

Now Summer, I slept on the forest floor
as I softened to each pine needle and cone.

From my slumbering mouth, silent verbs
came gushing as the still boulders on a quiet ocean's day.

I felt the sauces of the dashing rain which flashed
across the midday sky.

~

Walking home, I spoke to the giggling ferns
and softly brushed my hands across edge and flutter.

Donny Barilla

Covered as the Fog Lifts

The covered bridge stitched it's way from edge to edge.
Each splintered board rattled in enthusiasm.
I could hear the moans of the tunneling wind
as it passed the open gape of the ruddy colored pass.

Dancing leaves clamored about the caked dirt road.
Walking, I stumbled for a moment
as the crows leered at me in unison.

I looked to the sky and watched the thinning clouds
dry themselves upon the clever breath
of Summer's mist, clinging.

I walk on roadside for an hour -perhaps more.

The sun opened itself in all it's noble nudity,
prowling the Earth in gold and yellows.

The bridge rattled as the posture of rail and wood trembled
like a steamed teapot. The fog lifted.

Wintery Quilts

Powdered pollens dusted across the field
cut and threshed, I stood close to the edge
of this meadow, quiet and alive.

By midday, the snowy drifts paused in surmounting chills
which throbbed through my legs, ankles, and all
corners of these ancient bones.

I wandered through the clay wrapped rocks.
Ice clung to the stalk, quivering about the Wintery breeze.

Today, the sun was silent.
I tugged through the field
and listened to each snap of wood and long dead leaves.

The crunching wind whispered about my ears.
Finding a trail, I wandered for a time, open to the distant rising hills.

Donny Barilla

Genesis

Mosses swallowed the trickling tributaries
pooling about as the dancing greens of the onion sprout
throbbed its root quickly into the earth.

Watery bleeding fastened to the mud
tamped by the great bow of the maple
which cooled the hot forming clays, spread and cracked.

Leathers of my ancient skin poised as a canvas
searching for the mid hour sun.

I knelt to the creek and felt the tugging passages
of my throat host the cool water in a deliverance.

Now, at the hour so crumbled, I heard the ripples
of the brook mesh with grass. I lay open beneath

the flash of the sky
and watched the pinks swab across heaven's dome.

Dead Tongues

After a moment, once I soon arrived,
the old tree fell
and coughed across the dead Winter earth.

Stepping across the thick bark hide,
I crunched a certain leafy pile
and listened to the moans of a throaty chill,
beginning in the evenings shadowy grave

reaching upon the white gathered gown
which sulked and whimpered.

Slapping wind stung my face
as each wave of granules, snow drift,
weened me from the open glen
where ice spoke in dead tongues.

Donny Barilla

Winter's Gambit

The mountain threw a jagged crest upon the stomach
of the soft apricot sky.

I wilted in the patterning rains
which sulked about the white caps,

standing as still as a sentinel.

~

Wind charged across each rock and snowy fiber.

I sent my breath in a search for the more humid, warm air.

Into the thick of the stretching valley,

homes, cottages, and ancient farmhouses

scattered through with precise trim.

Dusty snow drifts combed through the sparse trees.

~

DANCE UPON THE FOREST FLOOR

I held my vision steady in a peering glance.
I took treasures from the mourning, dripping sky.

Ice fell upon my beard and hair.
The heat of my reddened flesh surrender to Februaries prison.

Donny Barilla

Cantor in the Deep of Night

From the silent, soft wools beneath her, I traced
the trembling caps of my fingers across the base
of her wheat and barley.

I reached upon her and I heard the distant
moaning from a distant ocean
which swelled about her nape and trellised
across the glaze of her lip and moisture from her mouth.

She slept through the night.
She slept through every night.
I could hear the crows nestle, preparing for tomorrows hunt.

Roaming gestures of the slithering foam
lathered upon the creamed colors of her thighs.

I lay beside her as I sculpted across the curves
which sang a silent tune in which only I could hear.

Into the Fey

I stretched, reaching my arms into the thick woods of the fey.
Removing blackberries, blackbirds, and salves
which smelled of peach nectar, I fevered at the dark swallow
of the wooded skyline.

I heard the moans of each simple pleasure.
Small, flecks of golden light danced
through the narrow angle of my eyesight.

I drew a decadent kiss from the fairest maiden
whom threw lusty scents and slumped,
slept at the base of my feet.

I saw the pond where Narcissus lay.
I tossed a glance of 'Hello'
and in return, I found his smile
and the glaze of his eyes.

Donny Barilla

Shadows Break at Spring

Her back roamed as pastures,
dips and rock laden earth
were the leathers of her soft browned skin.

Her eyes, warm chestnuts,
danced upon me as I sang
in the valley of my chest

only to kiss her trembling mouth
and touch the softness of her pale, white breasts.

Opening, the clouds parted
and I watched the prismatic sky
pour forth from a once black touch.

Her thighs, sculpted in endless rows of quivering bounty,
opened forth with shadows.

By Spring, I could hear her crawl forth
from this cocoon.

Smiles spread across her face.

DANCE UPON THE FOREST FLOOR

Beneath the Pond

Beneath the pond, alive with the greenest kelp,
she slithered with opened hair
so full and soft it wavered
as the leaves upon each tree which surrounded
the water's edge -climbing and motioning upon the wind.

Her feet sunk through the basin of murky soot.
Trickling water beads threaded across
the crest and summit of her breasts.
She spoke to the murmuring trees as the fondest
buds opened in eager want of tamp and depresses.

Quick pounce of the rattling branches were her arms
as she stroked back the films, cool and crisp, like linens
where she slumped to the edge and pondered.

Donny Barilla

An Evening after a Heavy Blizzard

Last Summer, I slept by the pond,
so alive with kelp. Now-

I sack by the orange flames, smoke
tickles through the trees, remembering.

Sparks thread across the sulking snowdrift.

Arriving Just before Nightfall

Now Autumn, I look to the trembling forest.
Wildly, the branches crackle.
Pale yellow, the leaves wilt, roll upon the pine needle bed.

I mesh my way through the dirt trail.
Far off, I can see the distant mountain peak.

Donny Barilla

By River, By Meadow

The river sled through the valley, ripe
as the heavy weeds and sprouting flowers
spread across the bank, flooded in the softest mud.

Last year at this time, I stood here
fondly dripping each toe through the grazing waters.

Now, I fasten my bust against the spirited wind.
I could smell her, quite alive in the slouching
press of lilies. I turned, trimmed my way deep into the valley,
blooming in whites.

Lavender Bush

Your satin white sleeves sulked about your slender arms.
The bloom off your thick, black hair, fleshed full
in the jaunting winds.

She knelt to this altar of fertile, soft earth, stood and
handed me the blue petal of the lavender bush.

Touching her chilled hands, I-
spoke to her of passing, sulking through the Autumn
veins clustered about the sky.

A week later, I walked through the fields.
I felt the grass as they snapped and crunched beneath my feet.

Donny Barilla

Thicket of a Bruising Wood

Washing my face at the creek, I heard
a moan from deep in the thicket of the bruising wood.

It spoke of sadness as the leaves cluttered the soil of the earth.
The creak of the fullest arms, branches cried of old age.

The acorn, chestnut trees, gave the moss and velvet
soil a thudding gift.

Sorrowful, I leaned against the wicker white chip
of the birch wood, tapping my fingers and thumbs against the tree.

In a moment, the wind slowed to a crawl,
I heard their voice on a passing breeze.

DANCE UPON THE FOREST FLOOR

Threading My Way

Through the snow covered grass
and thinning sprout of weed and stalk, I stepped
as stepping on linens-
I entered a tree lined glade.
The dead rosebush scattered in scarlet's.
I trembled my way past thorns
and felt the dredge of snow tamp my back, shoulders.

Skies amassed in a gray painted submersion
while the thin trellises of fog weaved
as a blanket for the infants and toddlers of Winter's gash.

I watched the glaze,
stretched and paused.

Strong wind mumbled through the sky
and suckled me in chills as I threaded my way
across fine carpets of gentle white.

I see the flesh of the early Spring grasses.

Heavy my boots press.

Donny Barilla

Publishing Credits

Scarlet Leaf Review, "Lovemaking in the Winter Hour", "Pit and Pail", "At the Machias", "Summer Heat", "From the Tender Current", "Blouse and Gown", "Alone at Midnight".

GFT Press, "Shoreline", "Squall", "Arriving Just Before Nightfall", "An Evening after a Blizzard".

521 Magazine, "Clamor the Ground", "Buzz and Steep", "Nibbling Seeds", "Soft Smile", Hungry Flash".

The Avocet (A Journal of Nature Poems), "Summer Showers", "Boyhood", "Snow Dispersed",
"Alive in the Glades", "A Day in the Pastures", "From Orchard to Rolling Stream", "Searching the Pines".

Adelaide Literary Magazine, "Fallen seeds", "Stooped to the Lilac Bush", "Dreaming in Autumn".

Oddball Magazine, "The Death of Zeus", "Beneath the Pond", "Early Summer".

Harbinger Asylum, "Smooth Water", "Brittle Winter", "Comforter of Down", "Apple Grove", "Undressing."

IBIS, "Gilded Rays".

Literary Juice, "By River, By Meadow", "Thicket of a Bruising Wood", "Lavender Bush".

Neologism Literary Review, "Moonlit Leaves".

Outsider Poetry, "Autumn Compromise", "Remembering Youth", "The Fountain", "Evening Roams".

Xanadu: "Threading the Way"

About the Author

Donny Barilla, a poet covering the realms: human intimacy, nature, mythology, theology, and man's relationship with death and the departed, has been writing for over three decades. He writes daily and strives to renew himself as an artist from page to page and body of work to body of work. Very seldom does he take a break from writing as he views it as a full-time job. He lives a reclusive lifestyle and finds himself clinging close to nature and all her elements. His home state of Pennsylvania strikes chords of poetic depth about him as he finds loveliness from cornfield to meadow.

Whether it's feelings of love, intimacy, or a special closeness, he maintains the feeling that death does not take these with him/her to the grave. Emotions and feeling outlast the flesh of the human body. Human intimacy draws near an enigmatic spiritual passion which conquers all on the prismatic scale of experience. When speaking of mythology Donny says, "myths were created to make sense of feelings which are complicated by very nature. They are perhaps more easily understood through persons greater than oneself. As for theology, a disciplined aspect, incorporates quite finely with passions and secured poetic comforts.

In one of Donny's poems, he states, "Geese flood northern skies, mushrooms crop a blooming glade, her scent lingers slow." Here reads a wonderful example of how Donny incorporates sex and intimacy with nature. In truth he has always felt there is no real difference. There rests a comfort in nature which clearly exists on the same parallel as sex and sexuality.

Donny lives calmly and mostly to himself as he draws inspiration for Asian poets, such as: Yasano Akiko, Basho, Issa, Tu Fu, and Ryokon. Finding beautiful contrast as well as condensed, packed, short lines which fulfill the reader takes Donny on a spiritual journey. This, in turn, brings him to a enlightenment of a strong poetic nurture which he strives to duplicate with each poem.

As a general rule, but not always, Donny writes poems no more than a page. He feels the piece should be found, read, digested, and understood as a single experience. He also believes the sounds of the words chosen create the images, not the definition of the words. Therefore, clear images resonate through the palate of the reader. These ideas have the reader enjoying the poem in a more mysterious sense rather than a chore to probe one's way through.

Donny has written eleven books of poetry, nine of which were self-published. He has dozens of poems in journals and magazines, as well as twenty books in libraries (public and academic). He placed in a contest, the Adelaide Voices Literary Award, as top finalist. He has hosted six poetry readings and two book signings.

www.ingramcontent.com/pod-product-compliance
Lightning Source LLC
Chambersburg PA
CBHW030116100526
44591CB00009B/418